Panda Discovery Kids: Jungle Stories of Cute Panda Bears with Funny Pictures, Photos & Memes of Pandas for Children

Discovery Books For Kids Series

Kate Cruso

Published by InfinitYou, 2017.

Copyright Notice

© Copyright 2014 by Kate Cruise & Timmie Guzzmann

All rights reserved worldwide. No part of this book can be reproduced or distributed in any way without written permission of the author.

My Favorite Panda Quote

Yeah, well, I just ate, so I'm still digesting, so my Kung Fu may not be as good as... later on...
-- Po from Kung Fu Panda

Introduction

The reason why I wrote this panda discover book as part of my "Discover Book Series" is an important one.

Every child should know about the issues that relate to the giant panda bear.

The giant panda is probably the most powerful symbol on the globe when we are talking about the conservation of species.

The giant panda bear is considered a national treasure in China. For the WWF the giant panda has also a very unique significance. The panda has become the symbol of WWF and has been representing this organization since 1961.

It is true the giant panda bear is an endangered species and we must all help to save it.

This book will provide your child with all the facts, stories, and pictures that are related to the panda and having a better understanding of who the panda is, from where it comes, and how it relates to us humans. Your child will also discover many interesting, curious, and intriguing facts about the panda which will in turn help your child appreciate its existence.

After having read the book your child will be better able to understand why the giant panda is so precious to us humans and why we need to save the giant panda.

By reading the book your child will personally get in touch with some amazing panda bear moments and this alone is worth going through the discovery phase that this book is going to provide your child with.

In the end your child will know more cool things about the panda bear and this knowledge will enrich your child on a mental level because knowledge is power.

If your child is an informed kid, he or she knows more stuff which in turn will enable him or her to get into a deeper discovery process and this in turn will help raise your child's interest level making him or her more involved and engaged in life in general.

This active mental discovery process will ultimately lead to a higher intelligence level.

Once your child is knowledgeable about the panda bear, he or she can decide which way to go from here and he or she can truly start a positive mental relationship and friendship with this cute, chubby, and peaceful pal.

Who knows but maybe this information is going to be the basis for some of your kid's future initiatives. Based on information like this your child might engage his or her initiative for the cause of pandas at a later point in time.

Helping shape a positive future and helping shape the intelligence of responsible individuals who are going to care for extinct animals and who might one day bring their own resourcefulness, responsibility, and initiative to the table is part of the reason why I made it my mission to create this discovery series. The panda discovery book, however, occupies a very special place in my heart.

This is why I finished this panda book first because the panda cause is also part of my main priorities.

The panda discovery book, which is part of my discovery book series, is therefore going to precedent all the other curious and intriguing animal discovery books within the series.

As a mother of twin boys and a little girl, I know that I want to be actively involved in their educational process to help shape their visions, imaginations, dreams, hopes, creativity, and their positive involvement with everything that this beautiful world of ours has to offer.

I have set my goal to help kids envision and discover intriguing, amazing, and curious stuff that they find cool and that is part of our life here on earth.

Encouraging them to view life from a totally new perspective and dimension helps kids build new mental connections between things that they might not have considered before is what I want to achieve with my books that I am writing for children about animals, nature, space, and other related issues.

Going through such an active discovery process helps stimulate the active thinking and contemplation process which in turn increases a child's intelligence in general.

Involving your child with a positive, creative, mentally involving and stimulating, interactive, and responsive educational discovery process where your kid gets satisfactory answers back is how you help shape the intelligence of your child.

If you are letting your child explore new and cool things about a subject you are making an active contribution into your child's future! Such an investment into your child's future is the most valuable investment that you can ever provide your child with.

This book will empower your child to raise and get answers for questions like why the panda bear is endangered, why the panda bear is such an amazing animal, why it is important to save the panda, what your child can do to help the panda, and many more.

These are just some more additional reasons why this panda discovery book provides such an important contribution into your child's educational process and mental development.

Once your child is aware about all these issues that surround the panda bear, he or she will feel more enriched and in tune with the nature, the world of the animals, our environment, and our earth.

Helping to protect the valuable species that have been brought to us by mother nature is one of our priorities as human beings.

We as human beings can create a healthy balance and we as human beings have the intelligence to create a balanced, protected, happy and peaceful life between humans and animals happen.

As you can see there are many reasons why reading this panda book is an important step into the future of your child.

I wrote the book in the most positive spirit and my main goal for the book can be summarized as follows.

As a mother it is my responsibility to entertain and engage my kids with positive educational content. In my opinion as a former first grade teacher,

mother nature provides the richest sources of valuable content for a child. Human beings, animals, and plants are a good way to get your child started with the discovery process.

My kids always tell me that they love to be entertained while they discover something new at the same time. Learning about some cool new information is how they learn best and they love to consume a mixture of pictures, funny facts, stories, and the curious and intriguing side of a specific animal or topic that they are learning about.

I know from my own experience as an educator and researcher and from my interaction with children in general that kids love to learn stuff the cool way.

I listened to kids and took the responses that I got from them and it is my goal to surprise them with a real cool book series. This discovery book series

is basically inspired by kids. It is made from kids for kids. It respects the way kids like to learn.

I created this book series in a way that respects the way how kids like to learn because they told me what they find cool and groovy and I listened to them and included it.

The book contains lots of pictures, cool facts, and other curious and intriguing stuff that kids just seem to be fascinated with.

This specific discovery book is about pandas and therefore it fulfills a second big goal. This book can also be seen as a contribution to help endangered pandas and to help stimulate children to contemplate about the endangered species of pandas.

This book should raise awareness about this endangered species in the eyes of a child. It should help a child be aware that it is possible between humans to sustainably coexist with pandas.

Lastly, I want to stress that this book is there to enrich your child's spirit, imagination, creativity, hope, dreams, and vision about the wonderful world of pandas.

A child must know that he or she has a stake in such a global cause like the panda bears.

Reading about today's issues in such a positive and mentally stimulating way helps empower a kid's creativity, initiative, and interaction to create a better and happier future for a life in balance with the nature.

A child should also know that although the situation of the giant pandas is very delicate, there are positive news in regards to the recovery process of the panda species because there are human beings who act in a very responsible way that helps pandas to sustain themselves in the nature by extending the nature reserves and by developing new projects to help human beings sustainably co exist and live in balance together with this endangered species - the giant panda bear!

This is the result of joint effort between the WWF, some responsive governments and local communities and people like you and your child!

I truly hope that you and your child are going to enjoy the concept and the content of this book and I hope you get lots of valuable moments out of this discovery series.

I welcome every parent and child to discover the wonderful world of the panda bears - the cutest but sadly enough the most endangered species at the same time!

A History Of Lovable Panda Bears

Did you know that we Pandas are native to China? Yes this is true! We are known as a national treasure in China.

We "Giant Pandas" first appeared in China, millions of years ago. Yes, it is very hard to imagine such a long time, but we Pandas are truly ancient animals!

Look at us today we are huge, but it is funny to notice that the earliest panda bears were no bigger than house cats.

Over the time, we Pandas have developed to giant panda bears like you can see here on the picture where you can see us in one of our favorite positions: SLEEPING!

We pandas were originally believed to be a member of the raccoon family or the cat family.

Why this confusion you might ask?

This confusion about us actually happened because our early ancestors, the red pandas have characteristics similar to a raccoon.

We, the black and white pandas that you see most of the time, are also called the panda bear or the bamboo bear because we just love eating bamboo plants all day long and after sleeping this is our second favorite

Researchers found out that we, the giant pandas, actually belong to the bear family.

Funny story don't you think?

Well, know that you know a little bit more about who we are and where we come from, let's jump to the next chapter where we tell you one of our next big secret: Where do we love hiding and where you can find us hanging around...

Types Of Pandas

Did you know that there are mainly two types of us pandas? These two types are the giant panda (picture above) and the red panda (picture below).

Do You know me....

...Well, I am the giant panda...

You are telling me that You Did Not Know That I look like a Panda?

Well, let me introduce myself...

I am the Red Panda...

The giant panda is a member of the bear family and the red panda is a member of the raccoon family.

Qinling panda is a subspecies of the giant panda that is dark brown and light brown (rather than black and white) fur.

The Qinling panda is really a subspecies of us giant pandas. The qinling pandas were discovered in the 60s but not recognized as a subspecies until many year later. Disregarding the nominate subspecies, the qinling panda is the first giant panda subspecies to be recognized.

Yes, the qinling panda is also much smaller in overall size.

There are an estimated 200-300 Qinling pandas living in the wild, but this is just an estimation and this is not an exact figure.

Funny enough to note that the Qinling pandas also are restricted to the Qinling Mountains, where they live on hills that can be as high as 1,300-3,000.

Where Do Pandas Hide & Where Can We See Them?

Can You See Me?

I am hiding in the tree!

In ancient history, pandas were found only in several countries such as Burma, Vietnam and in china where they are naturally found.

But now a days pandas are to be seen in most of the zoos all over the world.

Even now, in southwestern China, they live free in bamboo forests.

The cold weather, mist and the rainy mountains comfort them in their home town.

Sadly due to expanding of human population the species is now restricted to a small area of mountain forests. In winter when the weather gets too cold they move, looking for edible bamboo and also to remain confortable.

Sniff sniff...and other Panda Senses

When you are looking at our senses, you can find out that our vision is poor and it is similar to the vision of a nocturnal creator during day time.

We are believed to have a highly developed sense of smell and hearing though.

We can know what is happening miles away by using ouur sense of smell.

Interestingly we also have an advanced technique of chemical signaling. This actually happens by a scent glad under the tail of a male panda. Our female panda counterparts have the same chemical in their urine. Through these chemical signals we are always able to know what is going on and we can not be fooled.

We always know the identity, sex, and health of our counterparts and we truly know our territory. Our senses are truly powerful and help us stay happy, safe, and protected all day long so that we can actually enjoy our freedom or do things like enjoying the smell of a fresh rose!

...oh how this rose smells wonderful!

How Do Pandas Communicate?

We pandas are considered to be very shy and peaceful animals. We spend most of our time alone in peace, resting, feeding and searching for food like bamboo. In captivity we pandas tend to be more playful and social.

Unlike other animals like cats and dogs, we pandas don't show any facial expressions, nor are we able to wag our tails and perk our ears to show satisfaction.

We communicate mainly through our strong scent marks and callings. Even if a fight breaks out, we always try to avoid it because we are peaceful animals. In a case where we can not avoid a fight, of course, we will fight back to protect our territory and freedom.

Another important thing to remember about us pandas is the fact that when we are cornered we have known to be pretty violent sometimes.

Especially mother pandas with babies can even be very violent in order to protect her babies from the enemy.

Male pandas also show to be aggressive during mating season when competing with other male pandas over females.

In the next chapter you will find out why in general we prefer peace over war...

Panda Moves & Defense

Let's take a better look at how everything works with us pandas!

We call it the panda factory...

Adult pandas weight 165-323 pounds and male pandas are slightly larger than female pandas.

Their teeth are very strong as an adaptation for chewing bamboo all day long.

Our digestive system is more similar to that of a carnivore even though we are herbivores.

Herbivores means that we only eat plants and leaves.

Therefore we have problems in digesting our food. To make up for this inefficient digestion we consume a large amount of food and bamboo each day.

This is our reason why we are so chubby and such heavy eaters!

Another important fact to look at is our defense system...

Here come some Ninja Panda moves...

Our sharp claws and ability to climb trees protects us from predators.

Also our strength helps us in fighting and our coat colour helps us hiding so that our enemies can not find and hurt us!

Mating Of Pandas

We pandas usually mate in the spring time when our senses are awake after the dull winter time. In the wild, female pandas usually mate with the dominant male in her range. I wonder why?

Yes, in the spring time we pandas mourn and grunt. We pandas are smart when it comes to mating and we also use scents to draw female and male pandas to each other. In order to attract male pandas, females also are known to perform a strange kind of a back and forth walk.

Did you know that our female pandas reach sexual maturity when they are around five years old? Male pandas on the other hand only reach their sexual maturity when they are around six or seven years old.

Mating only happens once a year with us pandas.

Now that you know how we pandas draw each others attention, let's take a closer look at how we pandas actually multiply our numbers...

Reproduction By Which Pandas Multiply Their Numbers

Like any other animal, we pandas, too, make panda cubs by a process which is called reproduction.

The females generally give birth three or four times in their life time. Sadly enough our reproduction is very low which in turn becomes a threat to our entire existence.

Usually, we giant pandas mate in spring time and then we give birth in autumn. A female giant panda in the wild could have around 6 cute little panda babies in her lifetime.

However, a female panda gives birth to only one or two panda cubs at a time.

If it is a single cub, the panda mother will take good care of it because we panda bears love our little ones and we are very social with them.

However, if it a female gives birth to more than one panda baby, the panda mother will only choose the strongest to feed it. She will abandon the other weak ones.

This is truly a sad fact about us, but we pandas also adhere to nature's rule: "Only the strong survive!"

Panda Baby Boom

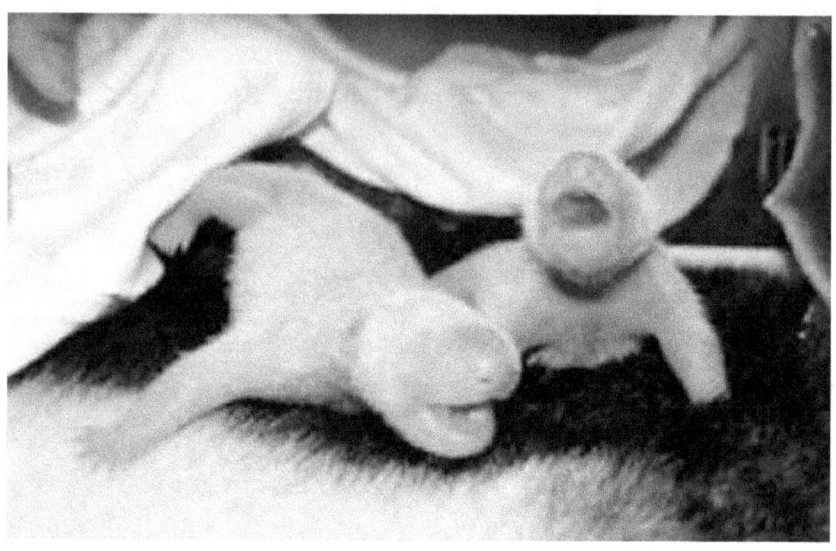

Hello world...look how tiny and delicate we are...

Panda cubs are very tiny with a body of only 15-17cm long and weigh around 36-296 grams.

Their eyes are tightly closed when they are born.

They are pink in colour and have tiny white fur all over their bodies. They can neither stand nor crawl except for a little amount of movements.

Cubs spend most of the day sleeping and suckling and they do not see the world with their own eyes yet.

However, a tiny panda baby can raise its head and make a loud sound as to let the world know that they were born.

It takes about 2 months for them to get the appearance of a grown panda bear. At about a week, black patches start to appear on the skin around their eyes, ears, shoulders and legs.

I told you we are very social with our little ones and the panda mother will not leave to eat bamboo until her babies are three or four years old.

They will only open their eyes to see the world with their own eyes when they are six to eight weeks old.

Panda babies will start to walk when they are about three months old.

Young pandas do not start to eat bamboo until they are at least one year old.

Looking After A New Born Panda Baby

In the panda world, the male pandas do not help the female pandas in caring for their cubs or in raising their babies.

The males go away after mating. They are leaving all the responsibilities of pregnancy and bringing up the panda babies to the female panda. Mother pandas, however, are better care takers than male pandas because they do take good care of their cubs.

Because these panda cubs mainly feed on milk, the panda mother will always be around the mother until the little ones are strong enough and mobile. The mother's warmth and body temerature helps the baby in regulating its body temperature.

Giant panda babies leave their mothers and start their own lives at the age of 1½ years. However, these young giant pandas still stay in their mother's home range for protection. At the age of 2½ years old, they leave their mother's home range for good and create their own territory.

A Panda's Mother love is universal and unconditional for her little one!

How Do Pandas Spend Their Day?

During day time we pandas are found mostly outdoors, but at night we sleep in caves or tree trunks. Especially when the sun is up high in the sky, we love to go in search for food, especially Bamboo.

Sleeping is our favorite thing and that is why we are called 'Lazy' because we wake up very late and we love sleeping during the day.

During the day, we take 2-4 short naps. The second most important thing in our lifes is filling up our tummies with yummie Bamboo plants.

We pandas love our Bamboos and that is what we spend most of the hours in our lives with! Eating bamboo is super fun and we are such heavy eaters!

Our average life span in the wild is 14-20 years, but expert scientists have found out that if we live in a protected zoo we can live up to 30 years or more.

Playing hide and seek in the woods...

Playing Pandas

Bon appetite...Eating Bamboo is how I spend most of my time...

Sleeping tight is my second favorite game...(ZZzzz)

Why not some playing with a mate?

...and finally playing hide and seek!

You have learned a bit of history about us Padas, how we love to play, eat, sleep, where we love to hide, and where you can find us.

In the next chapter we are going to reveal our secret number one to Panda happiness: the panda factory, our moves, and defense...

Panda Beauty

Yes we know that humans love us for our cuteness, chubbiness, and beauty. Don't we?

We are plump like a typical bear and we wear a thick black and white coat. Black fur is especially around our ears, eyes, legs and shoulders. The rest of our body grows fully with white fur.

We carry a thick and wooly coat that helps us in keeping ourselves warm in cold winter times. Our huge, round head is another sticking feature which makes us cute. We also have a tiny tail which is black in colour.

Up For Some Panda Playtime?

Yes it is a fact we pandas not only look cute, but we also have the best philosophy on earth which kind of represents our looks: "We love peace and hate war!"

...and that is why we pandas are most likely to exhibit friendly behavior and engage in social play in the spring as we warm up for the mating season.

Our daily fun activities include somersaulting, mounting, wrestling and playfully biting our ears.

Humans find this kind of playful behavior to be very cute and lovely because of our cute chubby looks and black and white fur pattern!

Next time you visit the zoo make sure you look at how we playfully interact with our mates...

Look at these 2 Panda wrestlers of the year...

...and at these 3 Pandas who are Football Stars!

Pandas & Bamboo & What Else Do Pandas Eat?

Our main source of food is bamboo like you can see on the pictures. I guess you can quickly understand just by looking at our pictures that we are true bamboo lovers and we take our eating habits pretty seriously!

In the forests from where we originated, bamboo was plentiful. Not only was it growing plentiful, but there were not many other competitor animals for this plant so we have been keeping it for ourselves.

The bamboo plant is our monopole and we decided that we should live on bamboo. Yes, it sounds kind of weird, but it is absolutely true!

Let me tell you, a wild giant panda's diet consists of around 99% of bamboo plants. However, bamboo does not give a giant panda enough nutrition. Therefore in order to get the amount of nutrition a giant panda needs, giant pandas have to feed on a large amount of bamboo plants. We giant pandas eat around 12-38 kg of bamboo every day.

Can you believe this?

Our bamboo meals consist of everything that a bamboo plant has to offer: the stems and the leaves of a number of bamboo species. We pandas just love our bamboo and we make no difference.

Another advantage that we pandas get out of our bamboo eating habit is that because bamboo is very strong, chewing bamboo all day long also makes our teeth strong.

Another funny thing about us pandas is the fact that we enjoy to sleep in bamboo thickets, too.

Bamboo is therefore our most favorite food and it is available to us all year round in forests that we live in.

Look at us! Don't we look like a bunch of flute players? But no, these are not flutes this is how we Pandas love eating our Bamboo!

Do Pandas Eat Other Things Than Bamboo?

We just had a big portion of fresh bamboo, but we are still thirsty...

In the wild, even though our main diet consists of bamboo, we also eat small rodents and grasses. If we are kept in zoos we are fed sugar cane, sweet potatoes, fish, carrots and apples apart from bamboo.

Bamboo, however, provides us with a good amount of water. Still we also need a good supply of fresh water every day!

Pandas & Nature

We love to mingle...the nature is our friend...and we are living in peace and harmony with the nature...

We pandas are not only very peaceful and cute animals, we also add beauty to the mother nature.

When looking at our interactions with the nature, it is important to note who our predators are. We do not fear a lot of enemies, but a few animals that prey on us pandas are for example the mean jackals and leopards.

But luckily for us we won't be a pray so easily.

We are smart, too, you know!

We know with our senses if another animal is trying to hunt us down and we pandas are fast runners. We are capable to run fast and to climb on trees. Trees are our true life safers!

Pandas & Us Humans

We pandas do not only live a longer lifespan if we live in a protected environment like a zoo, but we pandas are also well trained in zoos.

We are a very friendly species if we are kept in zoos because nobody can attack us and we love to live a peaceful life.

However, if we pandas live in the wild, like any other animal, we do fear humans. Today, more than 300 pandas di live in zoos and other breeding centers around the globe, mostly in China.

In these protected places, the humans do a lot to help us and to make sure that we pandas are well taken care of and that we are protected.

...and make sure to put out this message to others because we are an endangered species and we need Your help! Everybody around the planet needs to get this message!

On the other hand, humans can also be a serious threat to us pandas.

We fear humans who do not respect our freedom and rights. We fear the people who keep hunting us for our beautiful furs. We fear the people who hunt us down for their own benefits and profit.

Because there are humans who hunt us down and who sell our fur to others, we are now considered an endangered species.

The best way to help us pandas is by not buying any such products that are made from our fur.

Conservation efforts and breeding programs are in place to restore our panda population to a normal level.

Today there are animal rights and laws in place that makes hunting for our fur and destructing our habitats illegal.

Thanks for your engagement and initiative in putting out this message to everyone you know because you can make a huge difference! If everybody will put out the message like you do, our terrible endangered condition that we live in today might change for the better one day!

We love peace, we are peaceful animals and we enjoy our happiness!

If you love us pandas, too, make sure to defend us against these unhuman people who do not seem to care about us and who hunt us down for their own profit!

Thanks for sharing the message and thanks for being our fan and friend!

What You Can Do To Help The Panda

First of all you have to be conscious about the fact that species extinction is a totally natural process that happens over hundreds of thousands and even millions of years and it happens to every species in existance via a process called evolution.

The only thing that is problematic about the disappearing of a species is the speed at which it happens. Today, animal experts claim that the rate of extinction is between hundred and thousand times higher that normal.

This problem of extinction is directly related to the way the humans over-exploit the planet. This phenomen is also called the 6th wave of extinction by experts.

Let's take the giant panda for example. It is one of the planet's species that is threatened with extinction the most. If we do not take care of the giant panda it will be wiped off the earth forever.

The think that is most sad about it is that the panda is one of the most lovable speciel in the world. It is the symbol for conservation of nature.

By mobilizing people around the globe the panda might be saved. Today, there are individuals who feel very responsible for the cause of the panda extinction and they will do everything to help preserve the rich biodiversity, the plants, the landscapes, and the other animals that the panda strongly is connected to in order to survive.

The Yangtze Basin region where the pandas live provide some magnificent forests that are home to a huge wildlife and animals that the panda needs to be with. These are animals like the dwarf blue sheep, the colorful pheasants, and an array of other endangered species that include the golden monkey, the takin, and the crested ibis.

All these animals play an important role in the bamboo forests because they are capable of spreading the bamboo seeds and facilitating a greater growth of the vegetation.

The habitat of the panda is also the home for many other people. In fact, millions of Chinese people live there. It is also the economic and geographical heart of China. The goal is to make this area more and more sustainable which is also going to help increase the quality of lifestyle of the people living there.

Pandas also do bring a massive amount of economic benefits to these local communities because of ecotourism. Pandas do play a very important cultural role for Chinese people because they act as their cultural icon and heritage.

These are just some of the reasons why engagement and intitiative to protect the giant panda bear are one of the most critical priorities of today's environmentalists around the globe.

You can contribute to the panda's cause, too! Little things like telling other kids about this endangered species, reading informative books like this one, and refusing to buy any such products that are made from panda fur is a good start towards raising a global consciousness for this cause.

Thank you for your support!

Interesting Facts About Pandas

Yeah, That's Me?

Sleeping on the tree!

apart from Sleeping all day long here are some other amazing facts about me...

In china, pandas are a legend. Also we are considered to be a symbol of peace. In history, when human tribes were at war, warring tribes would raise a flag with panda to call a truce.

According to the legend, there is a truly amazing story behind us pandas and how we got our beautiful black and white fur coat color.

It is believed that we pandas were once fully white. In ancient China, when a girl was trying to save a panda cub from a leopard enemy, she died because the leopard attacked and killed her.

All of us pandas went to her funeral wearing arm bands of black ashes.

As we wiped our tears, we smudged the black ashes around our eyes.

When we hugged each other with sorrow, we got black color all over our bodies, arms, and shoulders.

When we closed we closed our ears when the cries were too loud, we got the black color in our ears, too!

Even toeday, we pandas have fans and are loved all over the world. The logo of WWF to protect our species exists since 1961. Pandas are truly a gift of nature.

Let's share the love for us and protect us!

I hope you loved reading about us Pandas and hopefully you like the way we are...to thank you for your love here is some Panda love that comes from us to you! We hope you'll receive our hugs that

we send you via this last picture...many, many Panda hugs from us to you!

About The Author

KATE CRUISE is a mother of two 6-year old twin boys and a little girl of 5 years. She graduated in Science Education from Cornell University.

Kate began her professional path as an elementary teacher and especially loved to inspire kids and interact with kids to increase their learning abilities.

Later she developed a true passion for research and this passion lead her to publishing her research about topics that kids are fascinated about like animals, the human body, the earth, the nature, and space.

Applying her pedagogical expertise and practical know-how that she has acquired over many years as a teacher, she takes her new career as a children's book author very seriously and calls herself the "Electronic & Interactive Discovery Mom Who Makes Learning Cool & Groovy!"

She also writes the science content for scientific blogs, blogs for children, and the content for many other publications online and offline. She publishes her content for kids in various different formats and for various different devices like electronic books, apps, physical books, newsletters, etc.

Today, she has written more than twenty books for children under various different subjects and at the moment she is dedicating her time to her latest book project that she calls the "Discover Book Series."

The first book in this series is dedicated to the giant panda bear and she is going to release more of these intriguing and curious fact picture books about the most amazing animals that live on earth.

These cool fact and picture books are loved by children because she has created the concept and the content of the Discovery Book series by letting herself be inspired by the kids themselves.

She listened to her own kids and to what kids find cool and love to learn about and this is how this Discover Book Series inspired by kids was born.

The concept of the Discover Book Series is as follows. Kids discover cool and groovy stuff that they find cool which brings the coolness factor to the discovery process and simultaneously they learn about a little bit more dry and factual stuff, too.

The combination of both is the key to success and it is the combination of both that makes them learn more effectively. They are provided with cool and funny photos and they get entertained with some amazing, curious, and intriguing facts about animals. The fun stuff combined with the more analytical and factual stuff is what makes kids learn more productively.

Kids love these picture books about weird animals and weird stuff that the animals are doing because they love the coolness and grooviness of the books and parents are super satisfied because their children show interest for things on a higher level as usual.

Parents love to buy Kate Cruise's discovery books because they love if their little ones are happy and willing to learn new things at the same time.

These discovery books make learning a very fun intellectual process because children are processing information quicker and easier and they also retain the information much better than with traditional boring textbooks.

A child learns faster and is enjoying the process of learning and parents are satisfied because they finally found a solution that works for both of them.

Parents love their child to be intelligent and smart and this method will make your child more intelligent in the end because it is a positive and interactive approach that works together with the brain not against it.

Getting a child involved in the learning and discovery process is key and once your child gets started with raising all kinds of questions you actually have done a great job as a parent because this is where intelligence starts to develop and grow into a totally new dimension.

If your child asks lots of questions you got the proof that providing discovery books to your child actually works because children who discover with their own senses and in an active and interactive way are able to develop intelligence on a much higher level than children who are not asking any questions and who are passively sitting in front of a TV all day long. Stimulation of thought increases intelligence and the brain power and TV kills the brain cells of your child.

Kate Cruise's Discovery Book Series makes sure that children develop a new dimension of intelligence because these books are very beneficial for your child's mental development and they accelerate the learning process so that your child learns quicker and easier and with more fun!

This is the true Einstein way of learning and this is probably how Einstein would have taught his own kids about the many fascinating facettes of gravity and the like.

Discovery books work in synchronization with your child's brain not against it like boring old and outdated textbook material.

Kate Cruise is a true Ninja when it comes to explaining conceptual, complicated, boring formulas, and hard facts to children and her discovery book series is going to enrich your child's life on a totally new level.

Today, Kate lives in Sausalito, San Francisco with her husband and her 6 year old twin boys and 5 year old girl and she is a true source of inspiration not only for her family but for many children and parents and homeschoolers around the world who are enjoying her books.

Parents and homeschoolers alike are reporting unprecedented results and they get results even with children who usually hate reading books and who have problems learning and retaining new and dry information.

Other Books In The Series

About the Publisher

InfinitYou is a hybrid general interest trade publisher. One of the first of its kind InfinitYou publishes physical books, electronic books, and audiobooks in various genres. Our publications are meant to educate, edify and entertain readers of all walks of life from babies to the elderly. Home to more than twenty imprints such as Infinit Baby, Infinit Kids, Infinit Girl, Infinit Boy, Infinit Coloring, Infinit Swear Words, Infinit Activities, Infinit Productivity, Infinit Cat, Infinit Dog, Infinit Love, Infinit Family, Infinit Survival, Infinit Health, Infinit Beauty, Infinit Spirituality, Infinit Lifestyle, Infinit Wealth, Infinit Romance, and lots more.